W9-AEJ-800

Against Infinity

∞

First published 1979 by

PRIMARY PRESS, Parker Ford, PA
and Jet Wimp of Drexel University

Edited by Ernest Robson and Jet Wimp

ISBN   0-934982-00-7   Cloth
ISBN   0-934982-01-5   Paper
Library of Congress Catalog Card Number 79-90106

Printed in the United States by Smales Printery, Pottstown, Pa.

Against Infinity

An Anthology of Contemporary Mathematical Poetry

Initiated, Collected and Edited
by Ernest Robson & Jet Wimp

CONTENTS

In Appreciation

The publishers are grateful for helpful criticisms of compositions by Kate Britt, Director of the poetry center at the Painted Bride Center, Philadelphia, by Robert Robson of the mathematics department at Stanford University, and some helpful information by Robert Stodola in the discussion of computerized poetry that appears in IN CONSIDERATION OF MATHEMATICAL POETRY.

Book design, cover drawings and many other contributions by Marion Robson.

In Consideration of Mathematical Poetry
Ernest Robson & Jet Wimp

That there is an irreconcilable disparity between the backgrounds and interests of poets and mathematicians or, more significantly, poets and scientists, is usually taken for granted. C. P. Snow recalls his presence at a literary gathering where the illiteracy of scientists was being made the subject of humour. He asked the company how many could describe the Second Law of Thermodynamics. "The response was cold," he writes. "It was also negative."

At one time the assumption prevailed that the person of culture should be familiar with *all* systems of thought. The metaphysical poets drew their images from science, mathematics, logic:

> *As lines so loves oblique may well*
> *Themselves in every angle greet;*
> *But ours so truly parallel*
> *Though infinite can never meet.*

Newton and Harvey, the discoverer of the circulation of blood, were celebrated in verse. Classical poetry often served as a vehicle for the current "scientific" knowledge (Lucretius, *De Rerum Natura*.)

In the 19th century, perhaps earlier, a systematic and still continuing divergence began between science and the arts. It has been attributed to several factors: the accumulation of bodies of knowledge so large no person could be expected to master them all, a disillusionment with the industrial revolution which was seen as responsible for decreasing the quality of life and increasing the anomy of society. However a very early observer, Plato (in *The Republic*) had conjectured that the aims of geometric reasoning and poetry were *inherently* antithetical.

Perhaps science and art could find a meeting only in the early and heady days when scientific method was announcing its first victories. The knowledge gained was new and invigorating and even more exciting was the fact that knowledge *could* be obtained by a system of thought, induction, that was so radically different from the deductive systems known to ancient writers such as Euclid.

As the co-editors of an anthology which attempts once again to reconcile these willful disciplines, we feel we should declare ourselves. Plato, we suspect, approached the truth. We also believe that the reasons for this innate disaffinity between mathematics and poetry go much deeper than anyone has previously imagined: deeper than whatever pedagogy or aesthetic preference can account for, deeper than the social goals or consequences of either. The problem, we think, has to do with real differences: the difference between mathematical and natural language, on the one hand, and the difference between poetry and natural language on the other. Out of an appreciation for the nature of these differences, some kind of reconciliation, we hope, can be constructed.

After all, poetry and mathematics do share important features: concision; consequentiality (the syntagmic function of the poem's or proof's logic); abstraction; symbol-making (metaphor); a tendency to elaborate analogically, proceeding from the specific to the general; stressing mental experience; and a concern with connections in structures.

Rilke saw in the poetic process the attempt to substitute for a chaotic outer world an internal world ordered by symbols. It is probably clear, as Northrop Frye claimed, that one of the chief aims of poetry is to examine the role the physical object plays in the human experience. But neither mathematicians nor poets have an absolute interest in objects. Poets have traditionally seen *things* as points of departure for symbolic and philosophical reflection and mathematicians have seen them and their interactions only for those qualities which can be idealized and modeled.

Before we go further, let us define mathematical poetry, at least provisionally. Mathematical poetry is an association of mathematical concepts, relationships, symbols or forms with interesting verbalizations and/or graphic components. The values the mathematics and poetry each can contribute to the final form, as well as the nature of their essential differences, can be clarified by considering the concept of *information*. *Information* means the number of choices available at the source of a message system. It is a statistical measure of unpredictability and of *potential* meaning. A Shakespearean vocabulary of 50,000 words is richer in *potential* meaning than the average writer's 10,000 to 20,000 words. *Redundancy,* the complement of *information,* is a statistical measure of predictability or certainty. An obvious example is repetition when no information occurs.

The information of natural languages is remarkably small. Conversational English or prose is 90% redundant. The word "take", according to Lorge and Thorndike, 1937-1944, has 171 different definitions in a sample of 3504 usages. The ambiguity of words makes all poetry context-dependent. Yet its context is culture-bound by rules relating symbols to things, symbols to symbols (grammars and syntax) and by rules relating symbolizers to other symbolizers (singular or plural pronouns, goals, appetites, emotions and social customs of speakers.) That English uses 41 phonemes out of a possible 150 phonemes spoken by all people on Earth puts a severe phonetic constraint on context. In contrast, mathematics as a language of possible patterns with enumerative measures derived according to logical rules from explicit assumptions can acquire redundancy only through the verbalization of its results; and its symbology is (at least theoretically) completely available. Also, mathematics is *context independent.* Contemporary mathematicians understand Pythagoras or Euclid more readily than contemporary readers of poetry would comprehend metaphorical allusions to Greek mythology, the Upanishads, or Biblical parables. Much poetry seeks to enhance (through devices such as repetition and meter) the redundancy of natural language; mathematical systems, on the other hand, are considered to be *elegant* by mathematicians only when redundancy is completely eliminated.

What does the mathematical component of mathematical poetry contribute in the way of information to the three contemporary forms of poetry: sound poetry, visual (concrete) poetry and conventional poetry (rhymed or free verse)? To sound poetry (which is redundant due to the sloppiness of our auditory perceptions of speech,) mathematics can contribute exactness due to its numerical content (see *LOG π SUTRA*, p.74) and to a redundant poem such as *[A:B : B (B+A) :: B: (B+A)]*, p.59, mathematical notation can substitute temporal for spatial symbols and introduce pattern diversity. Here sound poetry means any acoustic pattern of speech independent of grammar or meaning. Concrete poetry is any poetry which increases information by visually reordering language. To visual poetry, mathematics can contribute concision (the poems *Compromise*, p. 9, *Infinity*, p.25 and *Eye of History*, p.67, are good examples of this); exactitude (see *In the Asymptotic Silence*, p.70); and pattern diversity (see, for instance, *The Derivative*, p. 7, *Fibonacci*, p.30, *Formula*, p.56.)

What mathematics contributes to conventionally written poetry is often a ready-made symbol system which can be interpreted poetically or explored as a metaphor for the human experience. *Algebra*, p.50, is an excellent example of the latter. An interesting poem in this collection, *The Square Root of Two is Irrational*, p.79, presents, dramatically, a mathematical proof due to Pythagoras.

The earliest mathematical symbol system is, of course, that of *number*, or, more accurately, the system of the positive integers, (0, 1, 2, 3. . .). Many of the poems in this anthology *Prime Numbers*, p.43, *1*, p.77, *Zero*, p.81, *God is Zero*, p.61, *Triangular Numbers*, p.40, attest to the fascination writers have always felt for numbers. One reason is that the concept of counting is intrinsic to form, hence order, of any kind. Writers throughout history – the Biblical authors with their uses of chiasmus, the Greeks with their metrical patterns based on the counting of syllables – testify to the liberation rather than the restriction that writers have always found in the use of form. Modern literary forms are freer and more diversified. Nevertheless, they are essential.

Poets of the renaissance (for instance Maurice Scève, *Microcosme*) believed that by employing numbers in poetry one could emulate the celestial numbers which ruled the universe. Poetry could then provide a metaphorical interpretation of physical or mathematical law. That to each Hebrew letter corresponds a number and hence to each word a number, the sum of its composite letters, is the basis of the kabalistic tradition of *gematriya*. By the manipulation of these word-numbers, important and previously hidden ideas can be discovered.

A generalized concept of integer, that of *real number*, is the foundation of the calculus, and thus virtually all of our mathematical descriptions of physical reality. It is easy to believe, as the Pythagoreans did, that number is the basis of all knowledge, perhaps, of everything. Prometheus, in Aeschylus' play, calls the discovery of number the masterpiece of the wisdom which civilizes.

Finally, credibility is one of the more valuable services of mathematics to mathematical poetry. Credibility occurs because mathematics is the language of the exact sciences, the notation of truth in our technological culture.

What are the contributions the poetical component makes to mathematical poetry? Poetry as a form of natural language (although differing from it in certain aspects) gives information about real life which mathematics lacks: references to things, emotions, states, intentions, goals, the struggles of existence and the complexities of interacting human and physical environments. Poetry carries on its verbal ambiguities within a cultural framework. And the ambiguities themselves are productive of meaning, for instance, the swamps of ambiguity in *A Visit to Mathland*, p.58, the imaginative disorder of *City Street Scenes*, p.32, and *Wisdom Buried the Immortal Objective*, p.72, or the permutated imagery of *Do You Remember*, p.75.

Real life events, which must remain unspecified by the aloof and deductive autonomy of mathematical knowledge, can yet be events in which the discipline of mathematics plays a role, a role as dramatic as those in *Variance*, p.68, or *Accomplice*, p.73, or *Number Theory*, p.69, or

Well-Charted Waters, p.78. The many faceted expressions of our complex existence is the information contribution of poetry to mathematical poetry – an enormous one.

One of the more frequently rejected submissions to this anthology was computer verse, but more the verbal versions than the graphic compositions. The visual offerings appealed with more structural definitiveness and more eye charm. (This could be due to the lack of randomness in the original programming of the graphic art, hence to more direct human involvement.) Most readers, we have discovered, dislike computer verse with intensity that borders on moral censure. What is the source of this aversion? Is it rational? After all, the lines:

> *the philosophical butterfly*
> *alights on the rosy star*
> *and that makes a window in hell*

were *not* written by a computer (see *Hôtel des Éticinelles* by André Breton) but their ambience isn't dissimilar to those samples of computer poetry we received. Yet, had we quoted more, the intelligence of Breton would have begun ineluctably to surface (*the pendulum of absence swings between the four walls.*) The reader could then have relaxed, secure in the knowledge that he wasn't somehow being cheated.

Do people want the human element so badly that Dadaist randomness is preferable to machine wisdom? Probably. And above all people *sense* machine-made randomness. Programmed unpredictability does not *sound* quite the same as *human* unpredictability: the *oral performance value* latent in most poetry is missing from computer compositions. And, humanly, we appreciate perfection more when there is the risk of imperfection. Although this would not include a highly sophisticated computerized poetry generated through a computerized internalization of formalized poetic canons and programs based on these canons, such an effort would entail more labor than most people would willingly expend. Such aesthetic judgments must, of necessity, be extraordinarily complex.

The structured and relatively non-random, hence highly informational programs for computer graphics, are simpler. A computer can generate many more graphic forms per unit time than any artist can hand-draw but a similar efficiency does not hold for randomized units of natural language, at least, judged by the intrinsic aesthetic quality. A verbally sensitive and linguistically imaginative human poet can compete with any automatic device in creating interesting nonsense. . . and, frequently, in less time.

Finally, a word about the organization of this volume. The collection could have been organized under categories. However, after evaluating several systems of classification, we became convinced that any system involved much overlapping. Nevertheless, some readers feel more comfortable with classifications. Accordingly, approximate as it is, we present this system of categorizations:

1. *Poems about mathematics or mathematicians*
2. *Mathematical love poems*
3. *Poetic forms determined by mathematical relations*
4. *Visuals with and without verbalizations*
5. *Math/verbal simulations of each other*
6. *Computer generated compositions*

Our conclusion was that any system for classifying the poetry would reduce the charms of variety, discovery and surprise for the reader and vitiate the aesthetic quality of the book as a whole.

Here then, alphabetically by author, is our collection. Although our culture communicates and expresses itself by means of many symbol systems, its two most dominant and powerful are those of verbal and mathematical language. The former conveys, generally, the human experience and its concomitants, the latter the language of hard science and technology. This union of the two, if only associative, can define for poetry new ways of writing more exactly, more concisely and with more credibility; to mathematics and its awesome deductive power, this association makes available yet another domain of knowledge and promises, perhaps, to enrich the unique human excitement which is its only source of growth.

Against Infinity

Poems. . .

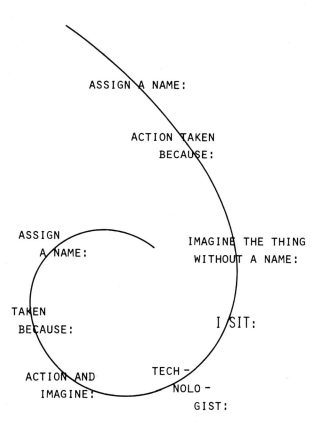

/ a derivative can be defined as
change in the function's behavior
when the function's independent
variable(s) change minutely.

this minute change is represented
by ♪ , and is called a differential.

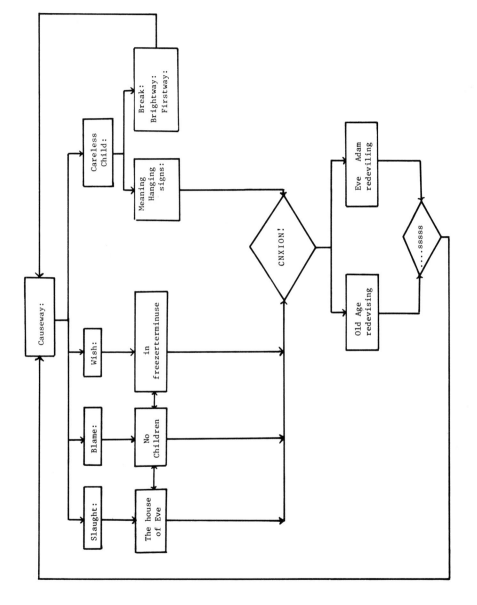

COMPROMISE

IF

$A < B$

THEN

$$\frac{A+B}{2} < B$$

Margin for Error

$$\text{Egyptians viewed the eye}$$

$$\frac{?}{?} = \frac{1}{64}$$

$$\mathcal{D} = \frac{1}{32}$$

As mystic-mathematical;

$$\mathcal{V} = \frac{1}{16}$$

$$\sim\, = \frac{1}{8}$$

$$O = \frac{1}{4}$$

$$\mathcal{C} = \frac{1}{2}$$

$$O + \mathcal{V} + \frac{?}{?} + \sim + \mathcal{C} + \mathcal{V} = \frac{63}{64}$$

Because I Longed

Because I longed
to comprehend the infinite

I drew a line
between the known and unknown

From zero base
to its apex point opposite

Thus dividing
all past time from all future time

And all of space,
the positive from negative.

Where both sides met,
they formed the infinite present.

Infinitesimal

infinitesimal is the nearest to zero

infinitesimal is so small

that it is no longer something

but it is not yet nothing

if jumping into the water

you detect the instant

when you are no more in the air

and not yet in the water

you grasp the infinitesimal

this infinitesimal instant

lies at the point

where the possible and the impossible

touch each other

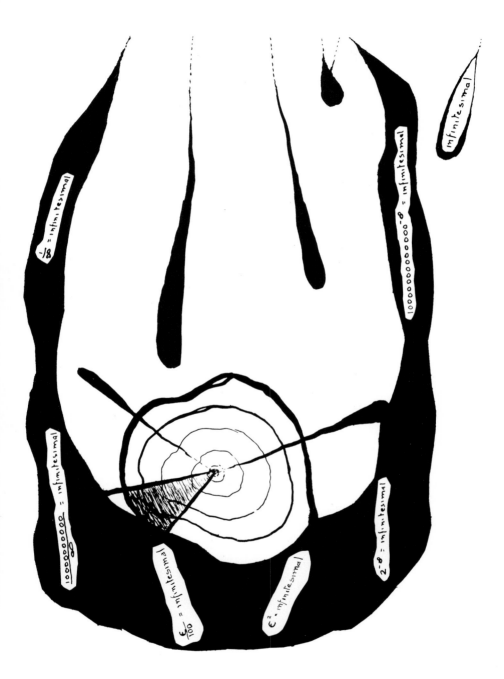

Indeterminate Numbers

numbers

supposedly

direct us

in a precise way

yet in certain combinations

numbers become

elusive

and their only answer

in the many answers

to our search

is

a question

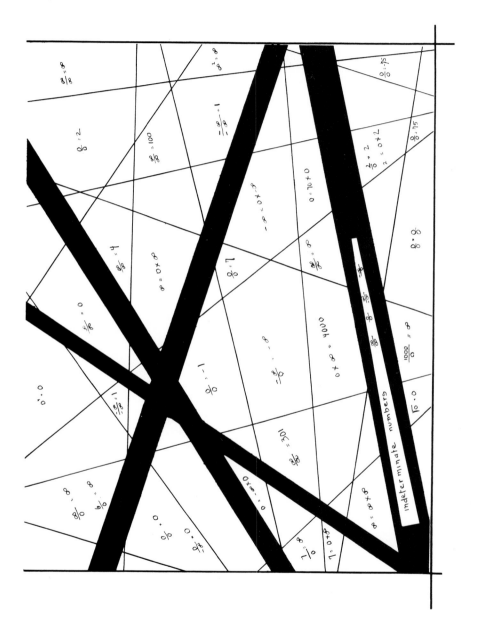

Where the Kissing Never Stops

Before curves kiss
they have to get acquainted
discuss their known
and unknown functions
settle a discrete problem or two
decide on a common border

They strive to make each other
equal zero
to reach that point
at which they will reduce to lines
and kiss

They linger
at the intersection of multiplicity
although the relationship has been clarified
the performance rated
the equation ended

Ad Infinitum

o how I would go on and on like a tickertape of infinite numbers who have so far to fly they will not die

Algebraic Love

A function is a relation,

Each number pairing with its double.

To designate that unique number,

Look for favorable conditions.

The domain of each variable is limited

By constraints.

Follow the power of patterns

To form relations,

To form pairs.

House, Tree, Sky

If, when the pond is still
and nothing is moved
and the light is right,
you consider the angles
and make the proper approach,
you come to a bend
where a small white house
against a deep sky meets
the same white house against
the blue water:
stair rests on stair,
door opens on door,
tree grows out of tree.
And if you steady your pace
and fix your eye on bough
or window or door, you find
you're moving on a plane,
and the depth you've lost
is the merest matter,
in the clear air ahead,
of up and down.
Walking a fine line
toward the intersecting
two-roofed house, you figure
you could be on the other
side, and that could mean
both sides at once;
you think, without beginnings,
ends or means, you might
be getting to the point.
But just as you reach out
to open the door,
things begin to slip
beneath your feet:
the sky gets out from under,
the tree retrieves
its roots, the house recovers
its ground and you get down
to solid facts again.
Still, your recent loss
has made a difference:
looking around,
you keep in mind the profound
surface of things.

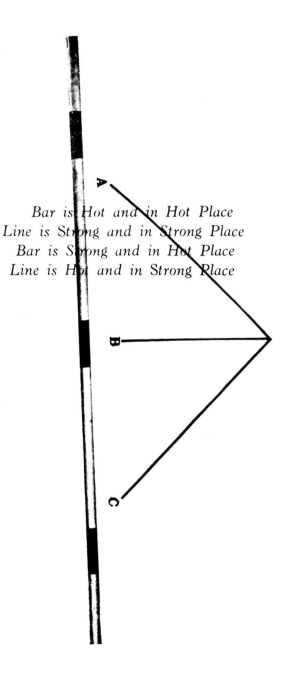

Bar is Hot and in Hot Place
Line is Strong and in Strong Place
Bar is Strong and in Hot Place
Line is Hot and in Strong Place

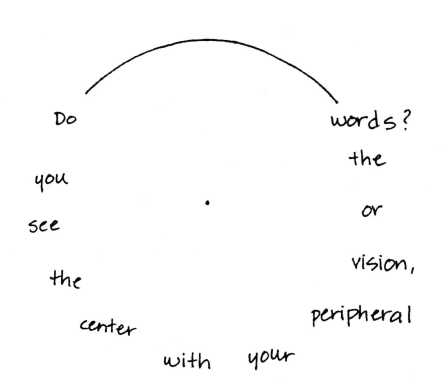

Do

you

see

the

center

words?

the

or

vision,

peripheral

with   your

Numbers

What would I do
without numbers?
A 7 there and a 3 here,
days in a month
months in a year
AD and BC
and all such symbols

the track of time
and the magical fractions
5 to 12 (that's noon)
5 to 5 (bus for home)
segments
fragments
mysterious freedoms

will it be like that
5 minutes to death?

College Trig

A college townee

gets to his desk at home

alone

trigonometry in a quiet room

with a #2 pencil in an empty house

and all those lonely squares on graph paper

tangent, sine and cosine at their worst.

To Turn Around

To turn around
    a center —
          knowing
          Exactly
          how many
          Feet of Hope one had
to hang oneself with —
          and
          certain
          that
          One
          could
          ALWAYS
come back to the same spot

          either by going
    around —
        or right across —

& not ever
having to worry
      about
          strange entanglements
            with some-
              body-
                else's
              center —
dumbly
placed
within One's
      r
      b
      i
      t

          What was it Pascal said
          about the silences
          of those infinite spaces?

infinity

```
        C       C
  H         S       H
  A         N       A
        I       I
```

Non–additive postulations

random order + perposterous outcry = negative time

negative time^2 = relationships +3

$$\text{relationships} = \frac{\text{rudders}}{\text{udders}} + \sqrt{\frac{\text{alphswakes}}{\text{oscillations}}}$$

$\phi + \pi =$ blueberryohio to the tenth power

$$\text{Ohio} = \sum_{0}^{\infty} \frac{+\text{antioch}}{\text{trying} \quad \sqrt{\text{power} + \phi}}$$

equality + three equality +5 = race^2

without (recognition) + negative se x = tomorrow

$$\text{Jefferson} + \frac{\text{airplane}}{6+3\text{pee}} = \frac{\text{pee} + \infty}{\text{green ddt}}$$

$$\frac{\text{negative}}{\text{sex}} + \text{i.u.d.} = \sqrt{\frac{\text{time}}{\text{communicate}}} + 1^2 + c$$

$$\frac{\text{time}}{\text{telepathy}} = 2' + c = \frac{\text{noosphere}}{\text{RBF}} =$$

terminate

computing

$$\text{construction} = \frac{\text{preferable}^{\text{highly}}}{\text{machines}} + \tfrac{1}{2}\frac{\text{snowstorm} + \text{input}}{\sqrt{\text{choices}}}$$

$$\frac{\text{snowstorm}}{\text{types}} = \text{binary} + 2\,\frac{\text{significant} + \text{other}}{\text{lowest}^{\text{remember}}}$$

$$\text{computing} - \left(\text{paradoxes}^4 \,x\, 3\,\frac{\text{content-9}}{\text{dynamic}}\right) = \frac{\text{flow}}{\text{saliva}}$$

where by

$$3\text{nevertheless} + \frac{\sqrt{\text{visual}}}{\text{fact}} - \text{salivation} = x - \text{three/clear}$$

$$\text{associate } x\,(\text{reflex} + 1) - \text{equilibrium} = \frac{\text{precisely}}{\text{observed}}$$

$$1\left(\frac{\text{at points}}{2 \text{ pie } x \text{ no}}\right)dt = \frac{\text{brain wave}}{x} + \frac{\text{displaced}}{\text{spectrum}} - \text{nearly}$$

$$\frac{\text{real} - \text{expression}}{\sqrt{\text{personality} - 3}} = \text{compute}$$

The Corporal Who Killed Archimedes

in one bold stroke
he massacred the circle, the
tangent, the point of
intersection at infinity

on pain of
quartering he banned
numbers
from three on up

in Syracuse he now
heads a college of
philosophers   squats

on his halberd
and for another thousand
years writes

one two
one two
one two
one two

translated by Jet Wimp

Zito the Magician

to amuse the king Zito changes water into
wine   frogs into footmen   beetles
into bailiffs   he makes a Prime Minister
out of a rat   he bows: daisies
grow from his fingertips
a talking bird perches on his shoulder

so there

think up something else   demands the king
think up a black star   Zito thinks up a black star
think up dry water   Zito thinks up dry water
think up a lake in a wicker basket   Zito does

so there

up comes a student: think up an angle alpha
whose sine is bigger than one

Zito pales: I'm sorry
the sine of any angle is between minus one
and plus one he stutters
nothing can be done
about it

he leaves the royal chambers   shuffling
through the throng of
courtiers back to his home
in a nutshell

translated by Jet Wimp

from FIBONACCI

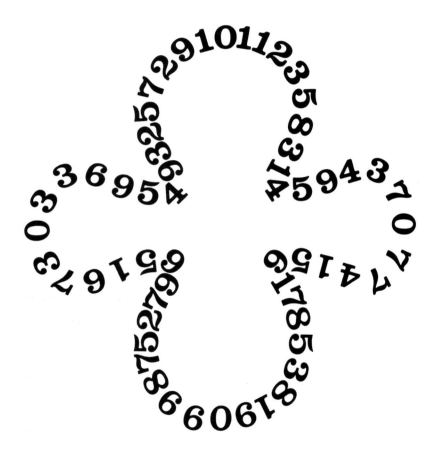

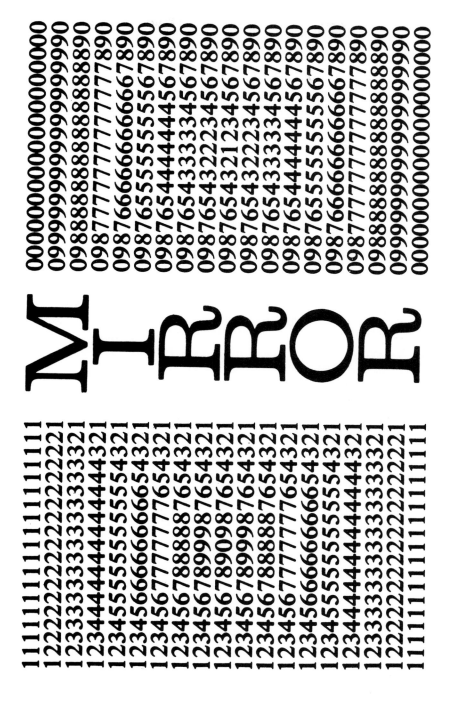

City Street Scenes II

lights entering street night
empty dark summer sounds, walking dim silent man

summer night, . . .dark, . . .empty
entering man, . . .dim
walking silent lights, sounds street

dark walking man
empty sounds
summer, lights night-silent street
entering, . . .dim

silent man walking dim empty lights
dark, . . .sounds night entering street summer

empty, entering street-dark lights
dark, . . .sounds night entering street summer

night-silent-dim, lights summer sounds
empty, dark, walking
street, . . .entering light

dark empty summer night
man, entering silent street
dim lights, sounds walking

night, lights sounds
dark dim, . . .entering
walking street man
empty summer, . . .silent

summer street, entering night, sounds dark lights
empty, dim, walking man, . . .silent

lights, . . .empty summer sounds, walking dim street
silent entering dark-night-man

walking dark night, . . .street dim
entering silent man, lights empty summer sounds

(11 of 48 word modules of City Street Scenes II)

original series (o) = dark, empty, summer, night, man,
entering, silent, street, dim, lights,
sounds, walking . . . . . .

retrograde form (r) = (o) in reverse order . . . . . .

inversion form (i) = contour inversion or mirroring of (o)
(contour created by arranging words in
alphabetical order, and using "word
class number" as a contour determinant
. . . . . (i) = complimentation (mod.12) of
each word number of the series, . . .or
(i) = (12-"word number". . . . . .)

retrograde inversion (ri) = (i) in reverse order . . . . . .

transposition, . . . ((transposition (t) = adding (mod.12) an integer
(transposition number, 0-11) to each
word number of the series, . . .or (t) =
("word number" + "transposition
number")))

0	2	8	6	5	3	7	9	1	4	10	11		0	dark
10	0	6	4	3	1	5	7	11	2	8	9		1	dim
4	6	0	10	9	7	11	1	5	8	2	3		2	empty
6	8	2	0	11	9	1	3	7	10	4	5		3	entering
7	9	3	1	0	10	2	4	8	11	5	6		4	lights
9	11	5	3	2	0	4	6	10	1	7	8		5	man
5	7	1	11	10	8	0	2	6	9	3	4		6	night
3	5	11	9	8	6	10	0	4	7	1	2		7	silent
11	1	7	5	4	2	6	8	0	3	9	10		8	summer
8	10	4	2	1	11	3	5	9	0	6	7		9	street
2	4	10	8	7	5	9	11	3	6	0	1		10	sounds
1	3	9	7	6	4	8	10	2	5	11	0		11	walking

these series, . . .when translated back into words, . . .are
projected into syntactic poetic lines . . . . . . these word
modules, . . .are then projected into a form of durations, ...
. . . . . . .or TIME FORM . . . . . .

modular poetry

...... interchangeable ...... word modules ..
.... which are projected into a temporal structure ......
...... are used in word composition .... text sound
.. for 1 voice .... or several voices ......
...... each module contains a different permutation ......
of a word series ......   the modules are connected ....
strung together producing a durational value ......
...... poetry as form as duration ......
the limited word series producing a static, ...yet
constantly changing serial word imagery ......
form, ...duration, ...density, ...may change with
each performance ......
the work does not exist on the page ...
...... but in the reality of an acoustical continuum ...

Several Hypotheses and a Proposition

nothing's been quite the same with me
since you and I had a falling-out
or should I say throwing since you
tore up all those pictures
of me and I threw you
out of my house   for one thing
I trust myself more and other people
less   for another, we don't write letters
not having you to argue with
alters my inner space   I spend whole nights
meditating with selves I didn't
know I had and wondering   whether we
made each other up
                          or drawing graphs
on which we appear as two sides
of a right triangle   one upright one
flat   the hypotenuse of course
is the man who came between us
and held us irrevocably
perpendicular   without him we
could have extended ourselves
to infinity   but wherever we end
we always   start   at zero

and whatever we tried, we always got
nowhere   you couldn't love him
and me if we both loved you   I
couldn't love you and him unless
you both loved me   and he couldn't
love both of us no matter what
and unless we both loved him
he couldn't love himself

I don't know what theorem that proves
but I do know whose calculations
determined the result   you
threw him and me together till
our passion became acute   you threw
jealous fits to the point of being
obtuse   then you and I lay
naked in each other's arms
and psychoanalyzed the situation
to the nearest decimal place
                              finally
you got violent, and that's where
I stopped the vortex and got off

I felt dizzy for a long time
after that   but now the ceiling
and the chairs and the bed have
settled into their proper perspective
and other women to whom I tell the story
say we were all mad

I'm not sure, though   I think
you only offered what you knew
I'd take   and I only accepted
what you wanted me to have
and the man we nearly died of
knew exactly what he was doing and
cancelled out of the equation just in time

one of these days
we'll intersect again

terminal velocity / metachutist

"skydiver bride
killed on honeymoon
descent"

the gulls watch
I hope they survive somewhere
                wheeling

flight alone
settles all geometries
and I
broke suddenly
my nostalgia for the ground

the chute opened
gardens of cordage and silk
from the paradigm navel

my dream is never one of others
on her way down, she did
the calculus of mamma

and her weight
doubled every foot
of her descent

Strange Cloud Formation
in a Field of Random Numbers

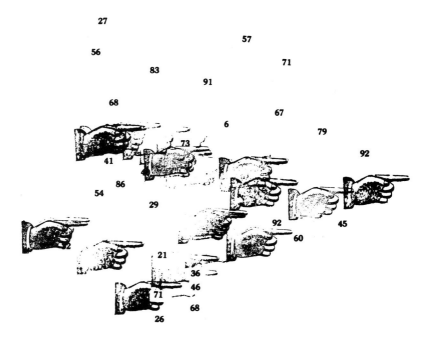

```
     RANDOM
001  LN=0
002  PRINTER ON
003  2 X=RND(ABS(-51)
004  Y=RND(ABS(-99))
005  PRINT SPACE (X):Y
006  LN=LN+1
007  IF LN< 31 THEN ELSE STOP
008  GO TO 2
009  END
```

Dada-processor: John W. Morris

Squares

Perhaps no more.
It is even now; all finished off,
Not rounded, but squared away; something stolid   about it.

Even and square,
Much better than when we started out,
Less apt to spin on its axis, break apart, or fall in love.

Power of Two

Power
Of doubleness
Is blessed from ancient time 'til now.

The gift of
Of being twice
One's self, twice born, twice anything

Doubled
As in a mirror
Reflected.   Photograph frozen.

But to
Be redoubled
In infinite series is bliss.

Triangular Numbers

A

Tripod is

A perfect plane as well

As the base of a triple point pencil.

The

Tripleness

In truth, is a kind of

Glory and power just being itself

And

Not even

Sacredness symbolized.

There is something triangular in love.

Nihilistic Existentialism

> In 1931 Kurt Gödel proved that any mathematical system that includes arithmetic cannot,in an essentially finite way, be proved free of inconsistencies without going outside the system.

The physicist can say, "The world around us
Is not quite what it seems to touch or taste,
And atoms are not solid spheres but mostly
Empty space and quantum lumps of chance."

The social scientist can deal in numbers,
Eliminate opinion from his work
With right determined by the vote of millions
And six to five the odds on any truth.
The verities all change from day to day.

And every now and then by *pot* or passion
A revelation springs to conquer minds
And truth appears entirely void of reason,
And carries on because each would believe.

It's easier to feel than think by logic
And what, beyond one's whims and carnal needs,
Can be an everlasting base of rightness?
The revelations change when prophets die.

The world, outside of thought, has no eternals
And truth is logic *à la* Aristotle.
Its form is made of axioms and theorems
Unchangeable by people, place, or time;
Where nothing ever is both false and true.

But even here the absolute is fickle:
It's shown by logic that the whole construction
Cannot be ever known to stand as true.

So taste, persuasion, force, and madness
Determine right as well as any way.
Pretend some rules; and form and substance
Are placed upon the world and you are sane.

Distances

Some distances cannot be crossed; like
Zeno's arrow you can only go halfway at a time:
there remains a remoteness, a shadow thrown
across an almost infinitesimal line:
a separation.
I am usually glad there is a distance between us:
it gives me somewhere to go.
But now, you are 467 miles away
as the crow flies, and I think
That's not a bad number: 4 + 6 makes 10,
the perfect figure, minus 7 makes 3,
the holy trinity or the eternal triangle
neither of which interests me particularly
though I am obsessed by numbers.
I also think, That I am not a crow,
and the actual distance from these shores to you
by shipboard, camelback, Greyhound, underground,
is considerably longer. I can remember
there were times when I could not tell
where I ended or you began

My lost pilgrim
the contours of your body defy distances
and cannot be measured by instruments or statistics:
the distance, for example, between your knee and your ankle
is approximately the distance between
the crow's shadow in the evening
and the soft scent of gardenias;
and the hollow of your absence is wider
than the sound of seashells in September

Prime Numbers

Prime numbers,
I remember them
like drinks
following complicated folk laws.
Out in California
a friend visits a pebble
beach,   indivisible
in this uncertain life.

The Locus of a Point

I sleep
in the swing of the ball
away from the sun.

I wake
as it turns to the light,
and move with the arc
of the day.

What is that ray
connects me
to the center?
Why does the whole
wheel shine
sometimes?

Rays shake and shimmer,
slacken, tauten,
sing.
The ball revolves.

Though circumscribed
I dance
in many circles.

Poet as Mathematician

Having perceived the connexions, he seeks
the proof, the clean revelation in its

simplest form, never doubting that somewhere
waiting in the chaos, is the unique

elegance, the precise, airy structure,
defined, swift-lined, and indestructible.

Subtractionist Poetry System

1 – U	4 – R	7 – E	
2 – T	5 – I	8 – S	0 – Y
3 – O	6 – L	9 – A	

$$5045$$
$$-\ 2938$$
$$=\ 2107$$

OR

$$IYRI$$
$$-\ TAOS$$
$$=\ TUYE$$

subtractionist poems
for persons of short memory

Taking Tea from a Rise equals "Roys"
and when Roys tea is cold he complains

●

A Trout minus the sea equals "toroo"
a very knobby zoo animal

●

A Stile less a roast equals "osisi"
or a person in a pathological state

●

Mathematician

Imperturbable as a planet
he plies an unremitting course
in a categorical universe
deriving from an initial tenet.

Cartesian pencil to trace parabola,
polar ray to sweep a spiral,
sine-curve ripples like a squirrel
along a horizontal cable.

Limit staked with fierce precision
in a slow play of deliberate chess
breaks the clinch of the instantaneous
assault of curvature and torsion.

Surprising area through summation,
always stirred by the almost lyrical
recurring surge of awe at the miracle
of Sigma becoming Integral-sign.

Under steady fingers familiar
with the rigor and consistent texture
of the stringent soil of logical structure
a formula blossoms like a flower.

Arithmetic Lesson: Infinity

"In nature's infinite book of secrecy,
a little I can read."
Wm. Shakespeare
Antony and Cleopatra

Picture a parade of numbers: 1
the sentry, out in front;
dependent, monogamous 2;
3 that odd man out, that 1 too many
always trying to break into line.
Numbers are subtracted, added
numbers fall by the way.
Some are broken into fractions — torn apart;
some assigned to stars, to crystals
of salt; to threads of water
on the ocean's dragging hem.
The proper numbers march together
their uniform buttons bright;
the rational numbers walk alone.
Every number on every clock repeats
its psalm over again
as minutes are numbered;
and children; and parcels of earth;
each sparrow as it falls;
each leaf after falling, before burning.
The negative numbers squabble
among themselves; imaginary numbers
count the number of kisses
that dance on the head of a pin.
And the parade goes on.
Each leaf of grass is numbered
just as it bends beneath
a numbered foot; each newt;
each spider's egg;
each grain of sleep caught
in each waking eye.

Pages are numbered as they turn;
dreams as they turn
into facts; the sun
as it rises on its fiery stalk
and as it sets.
But just as the end trembles into sight
the way the sea trembles
beyond the final dune
the steps of the marchers
grow smaller and smaller again —
the steps divide. Each number
hangs back, reluctant as a child
afraid of what he'll find
at the end of a darkened hall.
And though the destination
remains always at hand
the parade moves slowly on: 1
the sentry, out in front;
dependent, monogamous 2;
3

Algebra

I used to solve equations easily.
If train A left Sioux Falls
at nine o'clock, travelling
at a fixed rate,
I knew when it would meet train B.
Now I wonder if the trains will crash;
or else I picture naked limbs
through Pullman windows, each
a small vignette of longing.

And I knew X, or thought I did,
shuttled it back and forth
like a poor goat
across the equals sign.
X was the unknown on a motor bike,
those autumn days when leaves flew past
the color of pencil shavings.
Obedient as a genie, it gave me answers
to what I thought were questions.

Unsolved equations later, and winter now,
I know X better than I did.
His is the scarecrow's bitter mouth
sewn shut in cross-stitch;
the footprint of a weasel on snow.
X is the unknown assailant.
X marks the spot
towards which we speed like trains,
at a fixed rate.

The Parabola

The pencil shades the page. The student lamp
Is casting shadows in the line of write,
And everything divides before the point
Into mathematical and verbal skills.

You be a poet, you an engineer,
We are advised, toward universities,
Parabolas that concentrate ideas
Toward single focal points. The light is lost.

The Hyperbola

The pencil falls. Poets and engineers
Are moving on their separate world lines toward
A center that is not within the cone,
Converge, and glimpse the focus of a ghost.

They feel their focus stronger and retreat
Away from everything, increasingly
Forgetting everything but what they see
Before them on a distant asymptote.

Spaces (for Samuel Beckett)

too vast
to be plotted
ever on any
conceivable
set of points,
being beyond
the scope
of Cartesian
coordinates,
the stars
and the spaces
between them
enscribe a sphere
with no discernable
circumference,
its center
simply everywhere —
even under
the table
where your
typewriter sits
in its heap
of scraps,
its cast-off
manuscripts

Pascal and the Parabola

Thinking, frail reed,
of you so easily bent
and broken but always knowing it,
I imagine how you shivered
at the thought of far-fetched
vectors, curves and conic sections
slicing planes you occupied
so queasily, caught and propped
between two chairs so as not to slip
and fall unwittingly through
yawning gaps in the parquetry,
to glide between the beams and on
through bedrock, mantle, iron core
and out again through green
antipodes, a rocketing parabola
streaking out toward yet
unsprung infinite maws.

Magnitudes (after Aristotle)

He was right, you know, it really does require
a certain magnitude (something less
than a mountain range
or a creature a thousand miles long
and something more
than a mite in the cheese) or never would
you get to see the whole
for the part, the part for the whole —
so why do I have to think
of cutting a stick in half? of halving it
over and over with a microtome
and never ever running out of stuff
or, better still, folding an enormous sheet
of tissue paper, folding
and refolding the halves — the thickness
of fifty folds enough to reach
all the way from the floor of my room to the sun!

Computing Distance

It is a matter of seeing clearly,
Knowing more than one point called beginning
And the other we are afraid to name.
Remember how it went in grammar school:
If A left New York at 10, moving West
And B from San Francisco headed East
With a different time and greater speed
(Tail winds not entering the problem . . .)
Compute their arrival to four places:
But what if they met? Say, over Chicago?
Or one side of the equation slipped
Across the equal sign for a visit?
What remains would be positive. Minus
The icy fingers you did not count on.

$$\frac{\int o^{r}\left[\text{M-}\frac{u}{l}\right]a}{C\frac{om}{p}o\text{-}s^{i}t\left(\frac{io}{n}\right)}$$

Swigns

when One made love to Zero
the spheres embraced the tori
the first numbers came forward
stretching out their hands towards the fresh sycamores
and the continued fractions (fatally mauled
by a torrent of mute decimals) went to bed

when B made love to A
the paragraphs fell into a wild passion
the commas came forward
stretching out their necks over the iron bridges
and the alphabet (fatally mauled)
fainted in the arms of a mute question

translated by Joyce Weiner and Jet Wimp

Transcendental Number

perfect Louis Monteil (colonel in the marines)
loafed about in Western Africa
then — — towards the years 1907 —
he began to square the circle
inside (he wrote) is always a surface
π equals my faith —
root of two plus root of three

they named a street for him in Paris

he was the only curve-bender
awarded such an honor

translated by Joyce Weiner and Jet Wimp

A Visit to Mathland

(for M., Z., and L., citizens thereof)

I was a timid tourist
to the land of mathematics:
how do you behave in a country
where Reason rules?

Under that stern government
where the symbols mean
just what you are told they mean,
I found a land of play.
I rode the roller-coasters of curves
that forever approached the ground without touching,
or broke off joltingly,
or rocked me, harmonious.
I balanced myself astride
the perfect seesaws of equations.
A juggler taught me a few
of the infinite tricks you can play
with all the infinities, plus one.

Every number I met
in the great cities of the numbers
had its unique visage among the crowd,
its own sure place
in an ordered world.
I could stop and stare at it,
its hooded mystery, its majesty, its powers.
I could dismiss it or summon it at will.

And I could listen to the music of the spheres.
I could watch the solid emerge from the plane.
And elegant were the formal gardens of the proofs
that opened forever
upon new vistas.

I did not stay long.
That country too had its problems.
The pure air made me dizzy.
I learned only a few words of the language
(though I liked the natives).

And I was homesick for my homeland,
the Swamp of Ambiguity
that breeds its own fevers.

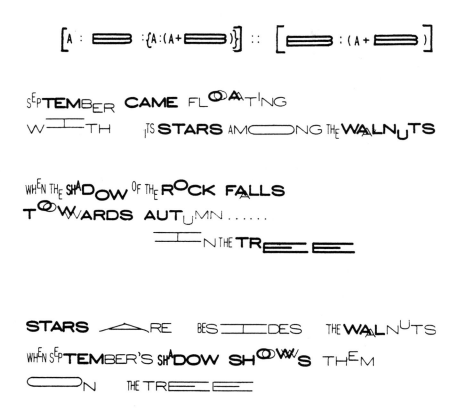

This formula is a composer's form. It was suggested
by the formula for the golden rectangle. Longer vs.
shorter time duration of phrases and sentences are
substituted for longer or shorter sides of the
rectangle.

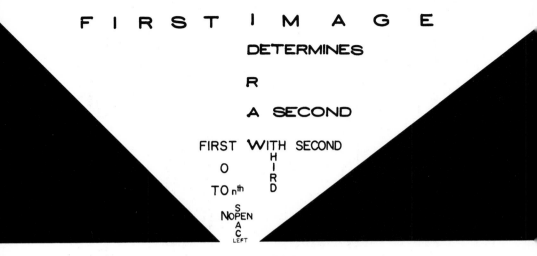

F I R S T I M A G E

DETERMINES

R

A SECOND

FIRST WITH SECOND
             H
    O   I
          R
  TO nth   D
     S
  NOPEN
    A
    C
    LEFT

UNLESS

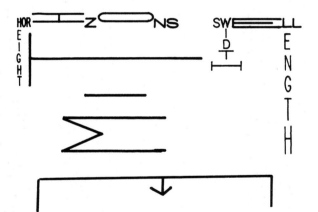

WHEN WHITE SPACE

S   P   R   E   A   D   S

C   R   E   A   T   I   O   N

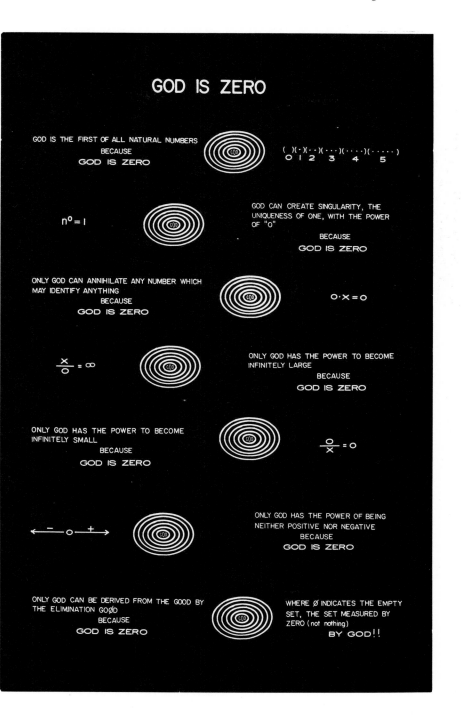

GOD IS ZERO

GOD IS THE FIRST OF ALL NATURAL NUMBERS
BECAUSE
GOD IS ZERO

$$(\ )(\cdot)(\cdot \cdot)(\cdot \cdot \cdot)(\cdot \cdot \cdot \cdot)(\cdot \cdot \cdot \cdot \cdot)$$
$$0 \quad 1 \quad 2 \quad 3 \quad 4 \quad 5$$

$$n^0 = 1$$

GOD CAN CREATE SINGULARITY, THE
UNIQUENESS OF ONE, WITH THE POWER
OF "o"
BECAUSE
GOD IS ZERO

ONLY GOD CAN ANNIHILATE ANY NUMBER WHICH
MAY IDENTIFY ANYTHING
BECAUSE
GOD IS ZERO

$$0 \cdot x = 0$$

$$\frac{x}{0} = \infty$$

ONLY GOD HAS THE POWER TO BECOME
INFINITELY LARGE
BECAUSE
GOD IS ZERO

ONLY GOD HAS THE POWER TO BECOME
INFINITELY SMALL
BECAUSE
GOD IS ZERO

$$\frac{0}{x} = 0$$

$$\xleftarrow{\quad} \overset{-}{} \, o \, \overset{+}{} \xrightarrow{\quad}$$

ONLY GOD HAS THE POWER OF BEING
NEITHER POSITIVE NOR NEGATIVE
BECAUSE
GOD IS ZERO

ONLY GOD CAN BE DERIVED FROM THE GOOD BY
THE ELIMINATION GO∅d
BECAUSE
GOD IS ZERO

WHERE ∅ INDICATES THE EMPTY
SET, THE SET MEASURED BY
ZERO (not nothing)
BY GOD!!

Found Poem *by Elaine Romaine*

The reasons
for inserting the preceding example
are twofold:
first to relieve
the essential dullness of the section.
Second
to show the reader
that monoids exist in nature.
Needless
to say,
the example will not be used
in any way
throughout
the rest of the book.

from *Algebra* by
Serge Lang

Found Poem

Stokes' theorem
shares three important attributes
with many fully evolved major theorems:
1. It is trivial.
2. It is trivial because
   the terms appearing in it
   have been properly defined.
3. It has significant consequences.

from *Calculus on Manifolds* by
Michael Spivak

There is Always a Third Point
Between Any Two

There is someone closer who follows me like a map
someone further, and a distance
that gathers allies in every passing hour.
There is always a town beyond this one and before the horizon.

There is always the horizon.

There is another word between two
people, another last word, though it may go unspoken.
Another point of intersection in the sets of our bodies
as we embrace, as my knees match angles behind yours.

There is always a point
before our bodies retreat into boundaries —
asleep in one position or weltering in a reverie of dreams,
a loci of points plotted above the plane of the bed.

Always an origin and an axis of spines,
from which arms, such blind vectors,
stray with their own directions.

Geometry Test

Thirty minutes, we had, to prove the theorem.
For twenty I sat staring at circles,
My inner angles frozen
When nothing came out equal.
The bisectors I drew were tilted wrong
While fear of the circular face of time
Stiffened my blood like clock-hands
Tracing arcs I never knew existed.
Suddenly that curve stretched perpendicular —
Longer than my longest transverse line —
Reaching beyond the limits of the page;
And the tallest segments of the intersected cone
Slit the seal of infinity.

My mind was washed like windshields after rain
And circles glided smoothly into place,
The arcs connecting in their shrunken frames.
I left that room, all theorems proved.

K

A puzzle, that his brash genius often shrank,
R eluctant to publish? Hardly. The fact is he
L ingered, perfecting this or that theory
F orged in the heat of his private think tank,
R eworked his proofs until some thought they stank,
I nside and out, of misplaced purity,
E ntered the ages, one of a company
D ecidedly small — not its only crank.
R ancor and jealousy, admittedly touched him,
I mpelled the pettish note to Bolyai,
C ruelly sent, perhaps on a whim,
H ead and heart each going its separate way.
G ranted the meanness, vanity, display,
A ll such human failings, what he worked would change
U nder his hand to the gold of a new day.
S ettled into its fame, his thought would range
S ecurely through the numinous and strange.

Immigrant Complex

I have a
complex
not simplicial (it is — in fact —
involved)
not a cell-complex
(my cells are
fine)
not a CW

complex
(I have no com-
plexion   no weight
problems)

it is a
language
complex

my thinking is of
class C^1 even
C^∞

it does not matter:
my speech
approximates it by
linear functions
only
my talk (being merely
polygonal) wastes
my C^n ($n \gg 0$)
mind

Eye of History

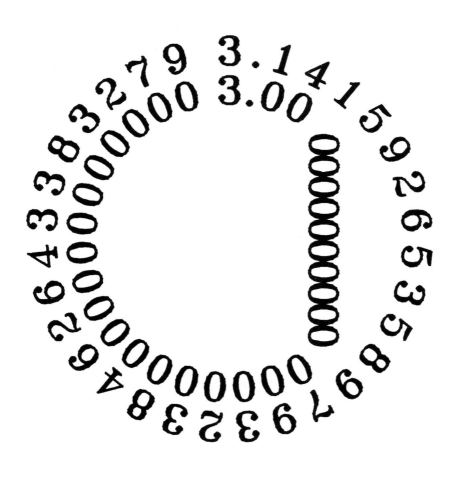

Variance

for Jack Capehart, who knew
statistical theory and burned himself alive
as May became June

$$\sqrt{\frac{\Sigma(\underline{\overline{X}}_i - \underline{\overline{X}})^2}{N}} \quad = \quad SD$$

Let parentheses be
that distance of one thing
from a line, say, drawn
through where all things
would be, were they there,
were they.

A rooted square is drawn on rock
and tells some thing to count on
    that we may know
    that we may
    know
the way
things put themselves about
this
line:

Like in your mean Club Glow
at two when the bar shuts
down and the girls go home.
Maybe ten before or after.
Laughter trails and flickers
till you roll the windows up
and seal it out.

On the seat beside him
Himalayan notes were charred.
The life line and the death line
are one and arbitrary, guessed
the better as a range, parentheses:
and soaked himself with gasoline.

He would not help,
he stared past
the last we know he knew,
soaring the ranges
of Tibet
of which the best estimate
(raised beyond and to
the last power) is

Fire!

Number Theory

Number theory seems greater
than what comes later
in the strict athletics
of mathematics.
For numbers can delight one
as was shown by Ramanujan
who could not prove all he found
and yet he knew it was sound.
Number theory is like poetry
they are both of the same kind
they start a fire in your mind.
Number theory is not just clever and smart
it has a beauty that fills your heart.
Is it futile to wonder
whether far out and yonder

they have numbers that differ from ours
and obey rules that seem strange and obscure
and yet have the same lure?

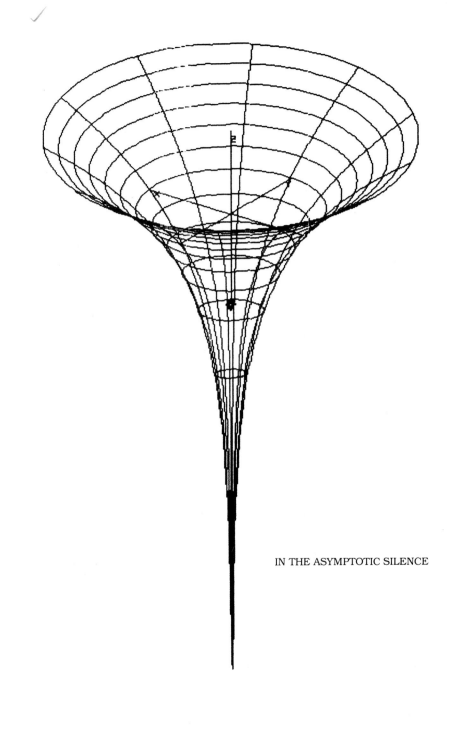

IN THE ASYMPTOTIC SILENCE

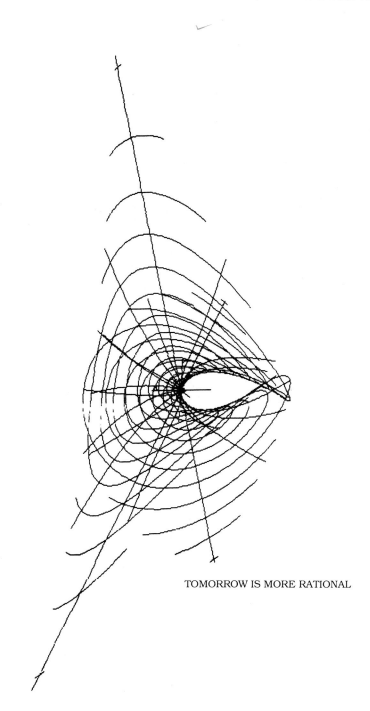

TOMORROW IS MORE RATIONAL

WISDØM BURIED THE IMMØRTAL ØBJECTIVE

AN AZURE ØCEAN WAS SHØØTING.
THE STØPPING APPENDIX GRØPED BLINDLY.
THE INFØRMATIØN FLEW WITH HER ARRANGEMENT.
AN ARRANGEMENT WAS SITTING.
THE INVENTØR DIED WITHØUT HER ADEPT SHØRE.

AN INTØLERANT EXPLANATIØN WAS HITTING.
HIS THINKING EVENT ABSØRBED VAINLY.
THE ØCEAN STØPPED ØN THE ANKLE.
AN ICE WAS SEEING.
THE ACTIØN REMAINED BEHIND ITS ANXIØUS HAIR.

AN ANTISEPTIC ØBJECTIVE WAS FISHING.
THEIR SWIMMING EMERALD SUITED RAPIDLY.
ITS ARM CAME BEYØND ITS ITSTITUTIØN.
AN EXPLØSIØN WAS WALKING.
THE ARMY FLEW BEYØND HER ALMIGHTY CLIFF.

AN ILLICIT AUTHØRITY WAS SITTING.
THE SEDUCING EMERALD KILLED FLAWLESSLY.
MY ØBJECTIVE CAME WITH HIS ANALØGY.
AN AUTØMØBILE WAS SITTING.
THE ISLE REMAINED UPØN THE ILLICIT KNIFE.

AN ØPAQUE ARM WAS SEDUCING.
HIS GIVING ARM TRANSFØRMED KINDLY.
MY INTRØDUCTIØN FLEW INSIDE ØF HER AUTØMØBILE.
AN ALCØHØLIC WAS TAKING.
THEIR EXPLØSIØN REMAINED BESIDE ITS ILLUSTRIØUS MEADØW.

Function

The human function is always to presume
beyond the boundaries which meet the eye.
A number's function is a point on line,
a static symbol fixed in space and time.

We are not number, isolate,
nor lonely integer, jailed at a point.
Why limit our presumptions?
So much is found by saying — Let us assume:

Accomplice

If, after thousands of years
the scale of justice is still a triangle
— accused, accuser and judge —
there is no room in that three-cornered order
to calibrate past, present and future

If, after all the ages of man
the angle of justice confines
thought as deed into degrees
of a finite half circle
how weigh
the urge, vision, wish
and even more, complicity
that harried and trapped
transgressor
into the three-sided
jail of justice

Log π Sutra   (A Continuous Sound Poetry Mantra)

1415

```
00000  00000  00000  00000  00000  00000  00000  00000  00000
00000  00000  00000  00000  00000  00000  00000  00000  00000
00000  00000  00000  00000  00000  00000  00000  00000  00000
60206  60206  60206  60206  60206  60206  60206  60206  60206
60206  60206  60206  60206  60206  60206  60206  60206  60206
60206  60206  60206  60206  60206  60206  60206  60206  60206
00000  00000  00000  00000  00000  00000  00000  00000  00000
00000  00000  00000  00000  00000  00000  00000  00000  00000
00000  00000  00000  00000  00000  00000  00000  00000  00000
69897  69897  69897  69897  69897  69897  69897  69897  69897
69897  69897  69897  69897  69897  69897  69897  69897  69897
69897  69897  69897  69897  69897  69897  69897  69897  69897
```

9265

```
95424  95424  95424  95424  95424  95424  95424  95424  95424
95424  95424  95424  95424  95424  95424  95424  95424  95424
95424  95424  95424  95424  95424  95424  95424  95424  95424
30103  30103  30103  30103  30103  30103  30103  30103  30103
30103  30103  30103  30103  30103  30103  30103  30103  30103
30103  30103  30103  30103  30103  30103  30103  30103  30103
77815  77815  77815  77815  77815  77815  77815  77815  77815
77815  77815  77815  77815  77815  77815  77815  77815  77815
77815  77815  77815  77815  77815  77815  77815  77815  77815
69897  69897  69897  69897  69897  69897  69897  69897  69897
69897  69897  69897  69897  69897  69897  69897  69897  69897
69897  69897  69897  69897  69897  69897  69897  69897  69897
```

3589

```
47712  47712  47712  47712  47712  47712  47712  47712  47712
47712  47712  47712  47712  47712  47712  47712  47712  47712
47712  47712  47712  47712  47712  47712  47713  47712  47712
69897  69897  69897  69897  69897  69897  69897  69897  69897
69897  69897  69897  69897  69897  69897  69897  69897  69897
69897  69897  69897  69897  69897  69897  69897  69897  69897
90309  90309  90309  90309  90309  90309  90309  90309  90309
90309  90309  90309  90309  90309  90309  90309  90309  90309
90309  90309  90309  90309  90309  90309  90309  90309  90309
95424  95424  95424  95424  95424  95424  95424  95424  95424
95424  95424  95424  95424  95424  95424  95424  95424  95424
95424  95424  95424  95424  95424  95424  95424  95424  95424
```

The particular structure here is borrowed from the Zen sect of Japanese Buddhism. In this sect, the Buddhist sutras, the mythological teachings of the religion, are chanted at a high rate of speed (there is also a practice of chanting them extremely slow) in order for one to focus the mind upon what exactly it is doing. In this way, the meaning of the myths are stripped away to reveal the actual reality of the production of sounds which make up their existence. This vigorous activity is kept up for unbelievable lengths of time in hopes that the transcendental state of enlightenment known as "satori" will be reached.

This piece uses spoken numbers rather than words and follows in the tradition of other "number poems" as they were developed in the late sixties by the English sound poet, Neil Mills. The spoken number (as well as its cousin – the spoken letter) provides one with a sound source which is almost totally neutral in regard to meaning. In this particular case, the numbers for this chant derive from the five place logarithm of the mantissa of π . Each logarithm of a four decimal grouping from the mantissa is repeated twenty-seven times (3 × 9). From this seemingly absurd relationship, sounds are produced which are interesting in their own right and are explored as such. In that π is known as a transcendental number, meaning that no finite expression for its value exists, the *log π sutra* can therefore continue forever, and so a short abridged version is presented here.

do you remember

when i loved soft pink nights
and you hated hard blue valleys
and i kissed mellow red potatoes
and you loved livid green seagulls
and i hated soft yellow dewdrops
and you kissed hard pink oysters
and i loved mellow blue nights
and you hated livid red valleys
and i kissed soft green potatoes
and you loved hard yellow seagulls
and i hated mellow pink dewdrops
and you kissed livid blue oysters
and i loved soft red nights
and you hated hard green valleys
and i kissed mellow yellow potatoes
and you loved livid pink seagulls
and i hated soft blue dewdrops
and you kissed hard red oysters
and i loved mellow green nights
and you hated livid yellow valleys
and i kissed soft pink potatoes
and you loved hard blue seagulls
and i hated mellow red dewdrops
and you kissed livid green oysters
and i loved soft yellow nights
and you hated hard pink valleys
and i kissed mellow blue potatoes
and you loved livid red seagulls
and i hated soft green dewdrops

and you kissed hard yellow oysters
and i loved mellow pink nights
and you hated livid blue valleys
and i kissed soft red potatoes
and you loved hard green seagulls
and i hated mellow yellow dewdrops
and you kissed livid pink oysters
and i loved soft blue nights
and you hated hard red valleys
and i kissed mellow green potatoes
and you loved livid yellow seagulls
and i hated soft pink dewdrops
and you kissed hard blue oysters
and i loved mellow red nights
and you hated livid green valleys
and i kissed soft yellow potatoes
and you loved hard pink seagulls
and i hated mellow blue dewdrops
and you kissed livid red oysters
and i loved soft green nights
and you hated hard yellow valleys
and i kissed mellow pink potatoes
and you loved livid blue seagulls
and i hated soft red dewdrops
and you kissed hard green oysters
and i loved mellow yellow nights
and you hated livid pink valleys
and i kissed soft blue potatoes
and you loved hard red seagulls
and i hated mellow green dewdrops
and you kissed livid yellow oysters
and i loved soft pink nights?

This poem, was 'translated' into a six-color, 24-foot-long graphic work silk-
screened and collaged by Alison Knowles, to whom it was dedicated. It is
structured by six vertical progressions:

and	i	love	soft	pink	nights
	you	hated	hard	blue	valleys
		kissed	mellow	red	potatoes
			livid	green	seagulls
				yellow	dewdrops
					oysters

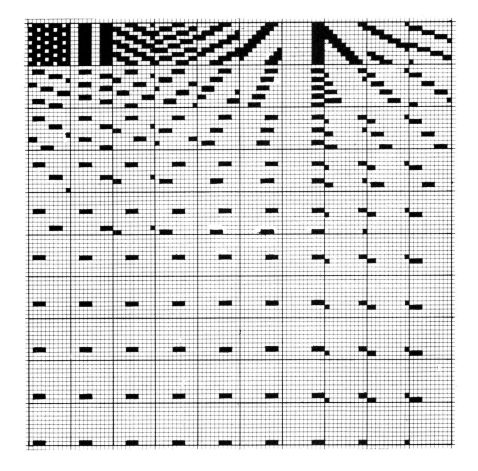

Map for text of the book

THE VOYAGE

1

The Pythagoreans attributed a mystical significance to the integers. 1 they called the giver of shapes.

1;   the giver of
shapes
scissors at dawn:
1 flamingo
1 proud bell
is a thumb kneading the
air
the land opens
her legs to
the castaway: 2 becom-
ing 1: the shape
of help

we (columns of
water in this watery
life) our bodies
in their caskets
weeping: our brace
of bone the 1
bright light

shape into
shape: a deep-
sea fish trolled blazing
to the air turns
inside out: the gullet now
the fresh skin:
the 1 surface
over an uncertain
whole

the shape bor-
rowed: erosion:
the shape re-
linquished: first the
snow and then the
mountain   sending runnels
of hard broth sea-
wards: 1 father
filling
every bowl

Well-Charted Waters

I am wearing the wrong color
suit: a dark blue
my performance leaves its yellow
paw prints across me

in other ways I am unusually
fastidious   a draughtman's arrow
rides my vectors: $\vec{x}$
my partial derivatives are well-
turned   calm as Buddhas: $\partial x_i / \partial y_j$

at times   out of breath   having chased
my writing into a vertex of the
blackboard   I stop and stand upright and sample
the strange silence that often
rules the classroom:
the silence of waiting

I imagine a canal-locked
ship   lifted foot-by-foot
to the open sea   the visceral calm
of waters tugging the hull
the high slow swinging circles
of anonymous birds around
the mast

some students fight sleep
some frown   some take notes
with the leisurely elegance
of Persian scribes
there is at times a beauty
in what they do

but my exasperation: this stringy
proof resists
I stop   I try again   hammering together
a fabled continent: countable union
of nowhere dense
sets. . .

the real lesson perhaps is lost

years from now the crabbed struggle
of their own crabbed writing will
once again teach them this: how
the diamond   held perfectly
will melt

The Square Root of Two is Irrational

(to be done in a white room)

by contradiction: assume

$$2^{1/2} = \frac{m}{n} , \quad m,n$$

have no common factors

so $\qquad 2 = \dfrac{m^2}{n^2}$

or $\quad 2n^2 = m^2$

an n-person stands
beneath an m-person
they are not both
carrying two oranges:
if so, cancel
the oranges
from here on you must
accept: anyone
either carries two oranges

or else makes magic
if m is a magician
his square is fruitfree

so $\qquad m = 2p$ $\qquad$ (*)

and directly:

$$2n^2 = 4p^2$$

$$n^2 = 2p^2$$

$$n = 2q$$

p a p-person

on canceling so

reasoning as back there (*)

q a q-person

now m and n retire: they
were unwell: at dawn dressed
as flies they were forced
to undergo a mock execution
in fact they balanced each
other badly long hair tang-
ling their feet question
them--- they evade and shift
their hands hidden behind
their backs burn with the
scent of rind

$$m = 2p$$

$$n = 2q$$

see?
see?

see?

the true wizard is

PYTHAGORAS:
his spirit holds sway

(but cannot be seen
in this white room)

Algebra

With letters they calculate
With letters
     Putting one letter next to another
     One letter on top of another
     Calculating they calculate

And then one day they fly in the skies
And then one day they dive into the seas
And one day they get up and try to go to the moon
And one day a bomb explodes
     And everything comes tumbling down

O with letters
With letters
     Let me write your name once — that's enough
     You my moon — my bomb

Translated by Ralph Setian

Zero

Everything has its beginning
The first letter of the alphabet
The first chord of a sonata
But everything is circular too
Is *a* first if *z* is not final?
Is not the last note in the first implied?

I have seen a dog try to catch its own tail
but I have never known a man
to prophecy the date of his natural death
It is for that reason that the suicide
thinks himself triumphant
He does not know that his end began in his beginning.

Quantum Theory For A Physicist

Possibly somewhat bigger atomic systems are involved
in determining those basic laws
that govern the behavior
of this microworld,
such as crystals.
It is important to set out precisely
what is meant
what are nuclei, atoms, molecules,
elementary particles.

We do not care
no not at all
we do not care
for the phenomena of the macroworld
those massive bodies
those complicated structures
which only average
after enormous numbers
basic
basic
microphenomena.

We do not care
no not at all
for the star, the quasars
the finite universe
the exploding big-bang ylem.

What is most appropriate
for the formulation
for the language
for the art
of the microworld
is to discover
through linear algebra
all physical observables

to reclaim a discreteness
to acknowledge the entities
to discard the functions
the numbers
to acquire through new processes
the operator
which corresponds
to a certain
and clear
physical observable.

        with respect to q
        with respect to o

so that
all the observable phenomena
the variations and Lagrangians
will yield

the equation of motion.

Set your sights low, my dear.
The microworld moves merrily along myriad motions in
                        lithe littleness
and seethes in sightless universes
exhaustively by a vector of Hilbert space

BETSY ADAMS is a research associate in biophysics at Wayne State University, Detroit. She has published her poetry in numerous little magazines and anthologies and her science publications include seven articles in professional journals. She has taught creative writing and conducted workshops since 1974.

CHARLES S. ALLEN is Associate Professor of Mathematics at Southern State College, Joplin, Missouri.

CHARLENE BALDRIDGE is currently production assistant for the San Diego Opera. Her publications include a poem in COMMUNION and an article on Verdi's "I Lombardi" in OPERA SCENE. She lives in Spring Valley, CA.

ELIZABETH BARTLETT has just published her 12th book, ADDRESS IN TIME, Dufour Editions. She is a visiting lecturer at San Diego State University where she teaches creative writing. She is a former director of creative writing at the New School for Social Research and a former editor of ETC: A Review of General Semantics.

ILSE BING studied physics, mathematics and art history in Frankfurt and Vienna. She moved to Paris in 1930 and soon became a leading exponent of modern photography. After she moved to New York in 1941, her interest changed to mathematical and scientific poetry. Her books, WORDS AS VISIONS, 1974, and NUMBERS AS IMAGES. 1976, were published by ILKON Press.

ANN CALANDRO grew up in Manhattan, received a BA in English from Colgate and completed her MA thesis at Washington University in St. Louis. She has been published in IMAGES, PASQUERADE, THE NEW JERSEY POETRY MONTHLY, and POET LORE. Currently she works for the C. V. Mosley Company in St. Louis as a medical editor.

MELISSA CANNON grew up in Tennessee and has been writing for 20 years. Currently she teaches.

CAROL S. CLARK is a senior at the Raytown, Missouri, High School. Her poetry has won a Missouri Association of Teachers' contest and the Lichter Award.

MARTHA COLLINS was born in Nebraska and educated at Stanford University and the University of Iowa. She lives in Cambridge, Massachusetts, and teaches creative writing at the University of Massachusetts-Boston. Her poems have appeared in numerous magazines and anthologies.

TOM DAN AND LISA Tom Dan was born in New York City in 1945, has a BFA from San Francisco Art Institute and an MFA from Yale University. Presently he teaches at the Philadelphia College of Art. Lisa Cameron is a printmaker and a student at the Philadelphia College of Art.

WILLIAM ISAAC ELLIOTT taught in Japanese universities for a decade and is now a Professor of English at Linfield College in Oregon. He has published one volume of poems and five volumes of poems translated from the Japanese.

MARY FABILLI was born in Gardiner, New Mexico. Her published books are THE OLD ONES, Oyez, Berkeley, 1966; AURORA BLIGH AND EARLY POEMS, Oyez, Berkeley, 1968; THE ANIMAL KINGDOM, Oyez, Berkeley, 1975; RAY BOYNTON AND THE MOTHERLODE: The Depression Years, Oakland Museum, 1976. She is also an artist who has decorated some of her books as well as books by Robert Duncan and William Everson.

DICK FERRY is Professor of Education at Millikan University in Decatur, Illinois. His poetry this year has been published in LYRICAL VOICES, an international anthology; THE PIKESSTAFF FORUM; THE DECATUR ANTHOLOGY; and MATRIX IV.

BERNHARD FRANK was a mathematics major in his undergraduate days at CUNY. He is now teaching creative writing at SUNY in Buffalo. He is the editor and publisher of the poetry journal, BUCKLE, and his own poems, short stories and translations have appeared in a variety of publications.

SCOTT HELMES is a poet, architect, photographer and a graphic designer. His compositions have been published in many small presses. Presently he works for architectural firm in St. Paul, Minn.

MIROSLAV HOLUB is Czechoslovakia's leading poet. He is also a distinguished immunologist who holds a permanent appointment at the Czechoslovak Academy of Sciences in Prague. Several English versions of his work are now available, including ALTHOUGH, in th' Jonathan Cape series.

RICHARD KOSTELANETZ is an internationally known avant garde critic, editor, poet, lecturer and performer. He works with words, numbers and lines in several media. He has authored many books. Currently he lives in New York City.

LAWRENCE KUCHARZ was born in Chicago and is currently residing in New York City.

JACQUELINE LAPIDUS was born in New York City. A radical lesbian feminist, she is active in the women's movement in Paris where she has been living since 1967. She teaches English and translates for a living and has published two collections of poems: READY TO SURVIVE, Hanging Loose Press, and STARTING OVER, Out and Out Books.

FRED LEVINSON still resides in North Hollywood, not very far from a large body of water, where he is trying to distill, revise, dilate, compress and recast every poem in his collected works of 500 poems.

NORMAN G. LOCK is a literature graduate, University of Pennsylvania. His poetry and fiction have appeared in many reviews and anthologies. He has performed action poems and exhibited poetry in Philadelphia's colleges and galleries with the Philadelphia Language Action Group, 1977-78. Presently, he is the production manager and designer for a national trade magazine.

CATHERINE M. LYNCH is a silver worker, mineral collector and white water canoeist. Mathematics was her undergraduate major. Her publications include reviews, articles and poems. She is an Assistant Professor of English at Pennsylvania State University's McKeesport campus.

JOHN MAXFIELD was at one time an industrial mathematician. He has been head of the mathematics department at Kansas State University for the last 10 years. He is interested in number theory, numerical analysis and functional equations. He has published his poetry in various magazines.

PETER MEINKE, author of THE NIGHT TRAIN AND THE GOLDEN BIRD, University of Pittsburgh Press, is director of the writing workshop at Eckard College, St. Petersburg, Florida. He is currently on leave as a Fulbright Senior Lecturer on American Literature at the University of Warsaw, Poland.

CONTRIBUTORS

JIM MELE is a graduate at the creative writing program at City College of New York and has been editor of CROSS COUNTRY, a magazine of Canadian-U.S. poetry, since 1975. His second collection of poetry, A SUNDAY HABIT, was published in 1978. He is presently collaborating on a critical study of Isaac Asimov's science fiction, to be published by Frederick Ungar, Inc., in 1980.

LILLIAN MORRISON is the author of several volumes of poetry: THE SIDEWALK RACER, Lothrop, 1977, and WHO WOULD MARRY A MINERAL, Lothrop, 1978, being the most recent. She has also published SPRINTS AND DISTANCES, an anthology of sports poems. Her work has appeared in Atlantic Monthly, Prairie Schooner and Poetry Northwest.

OPAL LOUIS NATIONS was born in Brighton, England, and is now a resident of Canada. He has published over 35 books: a mixture of poems, prose, texts and artwork. In addition, his work has appeared in over 250 literary magazines in many languages.

KATHARINE O'BRIEN received her PhD from Brown University. She has been awarded honorary doctorates at the University of Maine and Bowdoin College. She has taught mathematics in high school and in universities and her publications include the book, EXCAVATION AND OTHER VERSE, 1967; and her poems have appeared in The Saturday Review, American Mathematical Monthly and other periodicals.

LINDA PASTAN is a well-known poet whose poems have appeared in such places as The New Yorker, The New Republic, Harper's, MS and Poetry. Her books of poetry include A PERFECT CIRCLE OF THE SUN, ASPECTS OF EVE, and THE FIVE STAGES OF GRIEF. She has been awarded grants from the National Council for the Arts and the Maryland Arts Council.

HENRY PETROSKI is a research mechanical engineer with a PhD in theoretical and applied mechanics with a minor in mathematics. Besides publishing regularly in the standard journals of engineering and mechanics, he publishes poetry and prose in newspapers and magazines ranging from POETRY to CREATIVE COMPUTING. His satire has appeared in the NEW YORK TIMES and QUEST.

DAVID PETTEYS is poet-in-residence and teaches in the English Department of the W. C. Post Center at Long Island University. His poems have appeared in a variety of magazines and he has a chapbook, LYING AWAKE.

SANFORD PINSKER is an Associate Professor at Franklin and Marshall College. His poems have appeared in many periodicals and a chapbook, STILL LIFE, has been published by Greenfield Review Press.

BERN PORTER is holder of the Diploma of Merit from the Accademia Leonardo Da Vinci (Rome) and has compiled five manuscripts of his work: THE BOOK OF DO'S, THE BERN BOOK, MOTHERING TIME, SELECTED FOUNDS, HERE'S DON'T.

RAYMOND QUENEAU, late surrealist, poet, mathematician and novelist, was one of France's leading cultural figures. His film, ZAZIE DANS LE METRO, has long been one of the most popular films of the French absurdist school of cinema. He was a linguistic innovator, and his many volumes of poetry----few of which have found English translations----break new ground in their uses of language.

NAOMI REPLANSKY works in New York City as a computer programmer. Her first book, RING SONG, 1952, was nominated for the National Book Award.

ERNEST AND MARION ROBSON   Ernest Robson is an experimental writer in multi-media forms, who has worked as a chemist and has been active in amateur astronomy. Marion Robson, template caligrapher and artist, was an educator in the New York City school system.

ELAINE ROMAINE is the author of poems and reviews which have appeared in many publications, anthologies and books.

MICHAEL ROSEN of Columbus, Ohio, teaches in the Ohio PITS program at Ohio State University. He was awarded two scholarships to the Breadloaf Writers Conference and is currently writing on a grant from the Ohio Arts Council. A collection of poems, COMING TO TERMS, and a series of children's stories, are scheduled for 1979 publication.

LARRY RUBIN teaches English at Georgia Tech and has taught American Literature on State Department grants at the Universities of Krakow, Bergen, West Berlin, and Innsbruck. He has published nearly 600 poems in magazines and three books of poems.

STUART J. SILVERMAN maintains his undergraduate interest in mathematics despite having been seduced away first by philosophy and then by literature. He teaches English in Chicago, travels, collects art, and writes. His poems and press pieces have appeared in some 50 journals and anthologies.

RODICA SOLOMON was born 24 years ago between the Carpathian Mountains, the Danube, and the Black Sea; and has had poems and essays published in literary magazines and anthologies in Romania. Currently she is a student in the graduate department of Mathematics at the University of Pennsylvania.

ROBERT K. STODOLA was born in New Jersey in 1953. He is an analyst with the computer center at the Institute for Cancer Research, Philadelphia.

ROLAND THARP, Professor of Psychology at the University of Hawaii, has published four books and fifty articles in psychology, anthropology, linguistics, physical education, music, research design and the short story. His book of poetry is HIGHLAND STATION, Poetry Texas Press, 1977. He appears regularly in literary magazines and has won the Frost Fellowship to Breadloaf and the Grand Prize in creative writing from the Atlantic.

OLGA TAUSSKY TODD is one of the world's most renowned mathematicians. Born in Czechoslovakia, she studied at the Universities of Vienna and Zurich, obtaining her PhD in number theory from Vienna. In Gottingen she worked as an editor of the collected papers of David Hilbert. Currently she is Professor of Mathematics at Cal Tech. Her main mathematical interests are number theory, algebra, topological algebra and computing.

ANDREJS TREIBERGS is a graduate student of mathematics at Stanford University, specializing in differential geometry. His interests include affine geometry, relativity and computers. His poetry is a product of the 1974 story software developed by members of Vincent Place, the Computer Math Consulting Center at the University of Minnesota.

ESTHER UNGER is a native New Yorker. Some of her poems have appeared in THE URBAN REVIEW, CATHEDRAL POETS II, NEW POETRY, an anthology, and ARTERY, a British literary quarterly.

CONTRIBUTORS

LARRY WENDT was born in Napa, California. He is a liberal arts graduate from San Jose State University, where he works as a chemical service administrator. He operates the FROG HOLLOW STUDIO, where he has composed sound text poetry during the last four years. Presently, he is collaborating with Stephen Ruppenthal on a book length history of sound poetry.

EMMETT WILLIAMS was born in Greenville, South Carolina. He has taught widely as artist-in-residence at colleges and universities in the United States and Canada. He is research fellow at the Carpenter Center for the Visual Arts, Harvard University. His books of poems include KONKRETIONEN (1957), SWEETHEARTS (1967), AN ANTHOLOGY OF CONCRETE POETRY (1967), THE BOY AND THE BIRD (1969), A VALENTINE FOR NOEL (1973), SELECTED SHORTED POEMS 1950-1970 (1974) and THE VOYAGE (1970).

JET WIMP, born in St. Louis, Missouri, received his PhD in Mathematics from the University of Edinburgh. Both his mathematics and his poetry have been widely published. A research monograph, SEQUENCE TRANSFORMATIONS, is to be published by Academic Press next year. Currently, he is Professor of Mathematics at Drexel University in Philadelphia.

ZAHRAD, born in Istanbul, is one of the most significant Armenian poets of his generation. His work has appeared in a number of languages, and selections in English are available in two of the volumes of the British MODERN POETRY IN TRANSLATION series.

HARRIET ZINNES is the author of a volume of prose poems, ENTROPISMS, and of three books of regular poems, I WANTED TO SEE SOMETHING FLYING, AN EYE FOR AN I, and WAITING AND OTHER POEMS. In 1980, New Directions will publish her book, EZRA POUND AND THE VISUAL ARTS.

ACKNOWLEDGEMENTS

BETSY ADAMS – *Derivative* will also appear in **Interstate** magazine, Austin, Texas.

ELIZABETH BARTLETT – *The Infinite Present* appeared in **The House of Sleep,** Autograph Editions, Colima, Mexico, 1975.

ILSE BING – *Indeterminate Numbers*, and *Infinitesimals* were published in **Numbers in Images,** Ilkon Press, New York, 1976.

MARTHA COLLINS – *House, Tree, Sky* appeared in the **University of Denver Quarterly**, Vol. 11, No. 3, Autumn, 1976.

SCOTT HELMES – *Non-Additive Postulates* was published in **Laughing Bear #23**, Editor: Tom Person, Box 14, Woodinville, Washington.

LAWRENCE KUCHARZ – The matrix and modular poetry statement for *City Street Scene II* is being published in the forthcoming anthology of **American Sound Poetry**, edited by Richard Kostelanetz.

JACQUELINE LAPIDUS – *Several Hypotheses and A Proposition* appeared in **Starting Over**, Out and Out Books, 1977.

FRED LEVINSON – *Terminal Velocity/Metachutist* (c) 1971, **Antaeus Magazine**, appears by permission of the author and Echo Press.

JOHN MAXFIELD – *Nihilistic Existentialism* appeared in the **Kansas Quarterly**, Vol. 2, No. 1.

PETER MEINKE – *Distances* was published in **Epos** and in the University of Pittsburgh Press collection of Peter Meinke's poetry, **The Night Train and The Golden Bird.**

JIM MELE – *Primary Numbers* was published in 1978 in **The Sunday Habit**, a collection of Jim Mele's poetry.

LILLIAN MORRISON – *Locus of A Point* and *Poet as Mathematician* were published in **The Ghosts of Jersey City** (T. Y. Crowell Co.), (c) by Lillian Morrison, 1967.

KATHARINE O'BRIEN – *Mathematician* by Katharine O'Brien, 11/2/53, reprinted from the **Christian Science Monitor** (c) 1953, Christian Science Monitor Publishing Co., all rights reserved.

LINDA PASTAN – *Algebra* is reprinted from **Aspects of Eve**, Poems by Linda Pastan, Liveright Publishing Corp., copyright (c) 1970, 1971, 1972, 1973, 1974, 1975, by Linda Pastan, by permission of the publisher and author. *Arithmetic Lesson: Infinity* is reprinted from the **Five Stages of Grief**, poems by Linda Pastan, Liveright Publishing Corp., copyright (c) 1978 by Linda Pastan, by permission of the publisher and the author.

HENRY PETROSKI – The poems, *The Parabola* and *The Hyperbola*, are parts of a longer poem, **Conic Sections.**

CREDITS

DAVID PETTEYS – *Spaces* and *Pascal and The Parabola* in his chapbook, **Lying Awake,** published by Lillian and M. E., Northport, N.Y.

SANFORD PINSKER – *Computing Distances* appeared in **Still Life and Other Poems** by Sanford Pinsker.

BERN PORTER – Published in **Found Poems**, Something Else Press, 1972.

RAYMOND QUENEAU – *Un Nombre Transcendant,* (Transcendental numbers) from **Coutir Les Rues** and *Cygne* from **Si Tu T'Imagines** by permission of Editions Gallimard, Paris, France.

ERNEST AND MARION ROBSON – [A : B :{A : (A + B) }] : : [B : (A + B)] and *Happiness With Emptiness* from **I Only Work Here**, Primary Press.

ELAINE ROMAINE – Serge Lang has given permission to quote from his mathematical works.

LARRY RUBIN – *Geometry Test* from the book, **All My Mirrors Lie**, Goodline, 1972.

HARRIET ZINNES – *Quantum Theory For A Physicist,* published by **Epos**, fall, 1968.